PRACE FOR N
O

*Not Quite SuperMoms of the Bible* is a scriptural soul respite for every woman. I found myself laughing and learning from the brave women who have gone before us in their faith journey and inviting us, through their stories, to continue seeking God's voice above all else. A must read for any mom desiring truth and daily encouragement.

-Bekah Pogue,
Speaker and Author of *Choosing Real*

It's easy for moms to believe the lie that she must be a super-mom in every possible way. Becki's book breaks down the myth of super-mom by walking with us as we learn about moms of the Bible. She transports us into the time and mindset of that mom and breaks down God's truth into easy-to-understand truths. Her questions at the end of each chapter are simple and powerful. Every mom trying to be super-mom should read this book.

-Jill E. McCormick
Speaker and Blogger at
www.jillemccormick.com

Becki's perspective points out truth that most have never before realized. She brings women of old into 21st century living, allowing their experiences to come to life. After reading *Not Quite SuperMoms of the Bible,* you will no longer see these ladies as characters in stories, but as relatable friends placed strategically in Scripture for you to be encouraged by in your every day life. This book is my new "go-to" for baby shower gifts!

-Charity Berkey,
Founder, "Encouragement From Women
Who've Been There"

Becki is such an amazing and uplifting person. You will NOT feel as though you're the only mom struggling through this parenting thing. Her bubbly personality along with her desire to share Christ with others (especially moms) shows through each page of this devotional! You WILL love it!

-Brittany House

# Not {Quite} SuperMoms of the Bible

## REFLECTIONS ON LESS-THAN-PERFECT MOMS

Becki Rogers

Loved (5.5x8.5) Self-Publishing Template © 2017 Renee Fisher
https://www.reneefisher.com

Cover Design: Shelley Black
Cover Photo: Adobe
Author Photo: Sky McKissack

**ISBN-13:** 9781983059919

# Dedication

This book is dedicated to my mothers:

Marti Turgeon

Barbara Buchanan

Marriette Turgeon (1923-2007)

Wilma Gallagher (1928-2016)

And to my children, Asher and Ryleigh, who love me on both my SuperMom days and my Not {Quite} SuperMom days.

# Table of Contents

# INTRODUCTION

The stories recorded in the Bible were given to us as an example, right? They were people, with a real God working on their behalf in a real way. As moms, we often feel isolated, like we're the only ones going through our current situation. It's easy to feel that way, because motherhood, by nature, is isolating. No one else sees the endless hours spent rocking a fussy newborn, or praying over a sick toddler. No one sees the multitude of dirty diapers you changed last week or the last load of laundry you folded before your "baby" left for college. We don't get a glimpse into each other's real-life struggles, but we all know they exist—for you, and for me. And we all know motherhood didn't come with a guide, because if it did, we'd all have it tucked neatly in our bookshelf between *What to Expect When You're Expecting* and Dr. Sears' *The Baby Book*. All joking aside, there are many amazing parenting books, but none are customized to your unique family. Except one. And in its pages, we find "a Stronghold in the day of trouble," an "Anchor for the soul," and a Shelter to run to when the foundation shifts beneath our feet. There may be a season for every thing, as Solomon said, but let me tell you that if you don't get in the Word **before** trouble comes, you will not have sure footing when you find yourself facing a situation for which you have no answers. And as far back as Genesis, there have been mothers. Good mothers and not-so-great mothers. Godly mothers and mothers who chose to serve themselves more than God. They all serve to remind us that, throughout history, mothers have faced struggles that only God could handle. We have always needed Him and His Word. My sincerest hope is that in this study of the Not {Quite} SuperMoms of the Bible, you will relate and connect to each of their stories in a unique way that helps you, wherever you are right now. I promise to be open and vulnerable with my own failures and triumphs, and I hope that you will do the same in your answers to the reflections that each SuperMom inspires.

So grab your Bible and a pen and read on, dear Momma. And find hope. <u>You are not alone</u>.

# Eve

"The voice you believe will determine the future you experience." Stephen Furtick, *Crash the Chatterbox*

THERE WERE MANY "Not Quite SuperMoms" in scripture, but Eve was the first. Eve makes her debut on the pages of scripture in Genesis 2. At first, she was the answer to God's observation that Adam was lonely: her very presence solved the problem. Consider Genesis 2:22-25. If that's all she had been known for, history would have been so different! But most of us know that that's not where Eve's story ends. Now read Genesis 3.

The thing is, the ONE THING Eve is most remembered for in scripture happened before she became a mom, but it obviously affected her children--maybe in more ways than meet the eye. See, Eve walked with God, in His presence, every. single. day. Can you imagine that? Think of the last time you were in the woods. Was it quiet? Cool? There's a peace in nature that we can hardly find anywhere else. But now imagine an evening walk with God. God Almighty, the Creator of everything. For Adam and Eve, there was no question where they came from or Who they belonged to. Time spent with Father-God was part of their normal, every day routine. Did they take it for granted? Was it so normal that they didn't realize how special that was? The fact that they spent time with Him daily is a weighty thought, because in spite of that, Eve was still deceived by the enemy. Examine Genesis 3:4-6 again.

We can analyze all of the subtleties in that exchange, but really it comes down to this: she believed two lies. 1. God didn't really mean what He said, and 2. What she already had wasn't enough. The consequences were clear: separation from God, eternal death someday, and immediate banishment from the Garden of Eden.

So other than getting kicked out of the Garden, how did it affect her kids? Well, if you think about her sons, Cain and Abel, it's not hard to find that her son Cain believed that first lie as well. He thought that maybe God didn't ACTUALLY mean a blood sacrifice was necessary. In Cain's mind, what was the big deal? It was what he had to offer. But it wasn't what God required. And Cain's consequent murder of Abel brought another wave of grief to their mother's heart.

> We MUST shut down the lies of the enemy.

The second lie she believed, the lie that she needed more, is a constant struggle in our house. We don't have traditional cable television, but that doesn't mean my kids don't see commercials, advertisements, YouTube reviews, and various other media announcing the latest toy, video game, movie, amusement park—you name it. And they (my kids) aren't even on Facebook comparing their possessions to their friends'. Or, let's bring it home to us: we all have that friend on Instagram, right? The one whose home looks like it flew off the pages of *Magnolia* magazine—we **all** have that friend. Or friends, plural. We compare what we don't have almost reflexively, right? Poor Eve didn't have Instagram, and her only "friends" were Adam and God, but that's all the enemy needed. You may not need to go unfollow all of your unsuspecting friends, Momma. Just shut down the lies of the enemy when he whispers, *"My life would be perfect if my house looked like hers. She must have an endless decorating budget. Too bad my husband doesn't make enough money for us to move to a bigger house."* (I don't know about you, but the enemy usually whispers to me in first person!) Shut. Him. Down. Quote the Word. Start with Psalm 23:1.

As moms, it's our job to teach our children that God really means what He says, not only in what He asks of us, but also in His promises. It's our job to not only teach contentment but also to model it ourselves.

Teach them to hide His Word in their hearts so that they can fight off the lies of the enemy. Use Ephesians 6, and make it your family's own battle preparation.

Reflections:

Eve, and technically, Adam, blew it for the entire human race, all because the enemy caused her to question what God says. What are some practical ways that we as moms can help hide God's Word in our children's hearts?


In our American culture, contentment is not an easy virtue to develop in our children, and it's even harder when we struggle with it ourselves as moms. What can you do today to halt the comparison game and help your kids break out of the mold of materialism?


It may seem drastic, but trends like minimalism and tiny housing help us appreciate what we have. Maybe for you as the mom it means deleting apps or unfollowing friends that trigger discontentment in your heart. Whatever it is, commit to it today and stick with it. You have no idea the far-reaching effects it may have on your children and grandchildren. Eve is cheering you on, Momma! (See Hebrews 12:1)

Additional Reading:

- Romans 12:2, John 10:10, Ephesians 6
- Numbers 23:19, Isaiah 40:31, Philippians 4:11-13
- 1 Timothy 6:6-12, Matthew 6:25-26, 32-33
- Hebrews 13:5, Luke 12:15, Psalm 37:3-4
- Proverbs 16:8, 1 Peter 5:8-9, Matthew 4:4

# Mary

"The shortest distance between strangers and friends is a shared story about our broken places." -Lisa-Jo Baker, *Never Unfriended*

If there were ever a SuperMom in the Bible, surely Mary would be the one. Sweet, innocent Mary. The angel Gabriel called her "highly favored" and "blessed." Read Luke 1:26-38. Although it does not specifically say in scripture, my theory is that God would choose the woman closest to the Proverbs 31 woman to be the mother of His only Son. Surely she would be a SuperMom.

We know virtually nothing about Mary's life prior to Gabriel's abrupt announcement. There are things we can know about her, however, without a full life story in scripture. She obviously had spent time around God's Word---whether or not she read it for herself, she knew the promise of the Messiah. She knew and believed God would fulfill the

promise. Read Luke 1: 46-55. She spoke from
the overflow of her heart. This wasn't "new"
praise. This was tried and true praise. She
knew about the miracles of God over the
generations since Abraham--and she
recognized the miracle she had been chosen
to be a part of. Her heart belonged to her
Father. It didn't matter if she grew up rich or
poor or famous or unknown---it only mattered
that she trusted God. Her greatest
qualification for becoming what we would call
a "SuperMom" was...faith. Her response to
Gabriel was "let it be with me according to
your word." *Faith.*

And, when she could have boasted in her
supernatural calling, in all her SuperMom
glory, she didn't. She magnified God. She
called herself a handmaid, a lowly servant girl.
She gave Him all the glory. She saw herself as
God's servant, even in her role as a mother.

We can't help but elevate her calling: she
(presumably) cooked dinner every night for
the King of Kings. It's a high calling, for sure.
Yet, I can't help but wonder, do we see our
calling as less than hers because we raise
mere mortals? (Some days, they are more
than just "mere" mortals--some days they are
tiny, frustrating mortals. *Can I get an Amen*?)
But are we not His servants too, raising future
world-changers for His cause?

A servant lives to please her Master, waits
on His beck and call--bows to His every desire.
Can I honestly say I am His servant in my role
as a mom? Or do I feel ownership, like they

were my kids to begin with? Let it not be so! Just as Jesus came from the Father, our precious children are gifts from His hands, planted here in our lives, in our homes for a short while for us to raise, love, and nurture. And don't doubt it for one moment: you too, sweet Momma, are His highly favored, blessed servant. He trusts YOU with His kids. Magnify and worship Him in return and point those kids back to their Heavenly Father.

One of my favorite verses about Mary reads: "But Mary kept all these things, and pondered them in her heart." Luke wrote those words, but Luke wasn't in Mary's head. How did he know what Mary did or thought or felt? It's safe to assume that none of the writers of the Gospels were present at the birth of Christ. But a mom **never** forgets. I can still remember the mornings I took my pregnancy tests for BOTH of my children. I'll likely never forget the circumstances surrounding those exciting mornings! With my daughter, it didn't show up at first. I (naturally) assumed that meant I wasn't pregnant, but for whatever reason, I didn't throw the test away. I left it and continued to get ready for the day. About 30 minutes later, the test showed a very different result! (Who knew that could happen?! And it was correct, because the next spring we were holding a tiny little baby doll!) Regardless, I imagine that Mary spent quiet afternoons retelling the miraculous events of those early days of the prophecy's fulfilling. Whoever would listen—I can picture her pouring a cup of tea, inviting her listeners to sit at the table He built her while she told them what God had done in and through her all those years ago. Maybe her favorite story to tell was the time she almost "lost" the Messiah at the Temple—surely you have a CRAZY story you share whenever moms are sitting around swapping "war stories." Perhaps that's why that particular story made it in to Luke's account. I mean, put yourself in her shoes: God gave her the task of raising His Son, and *she can't find Him*!!!!! Ahh! I'd tell that story a lot too. I can picture her, taking a sip of tea as she lets it sink in, the enormity of what that felt like, and then maybe she says reflectively, "And that's when I knew that He was here on heavenly business, and His Father's agenda would always be His greatest priority." Mary had a front-row seat to the greatest time in human history, and yet in every mention of her, she was pointing all eyes to her Savior.

> In every mention of Mary, she was always pointing all eyes to the Savior.

Reflections:

What kind of shift in our attitudes has to take place for us to see ourselves as servants of God in our role as mothers? Do you see motherhood as a calling?

Did you know that you are highly favored and blessed by God? Your children did not get the mother they have by mistake. Yours is a holy calling. A deliberate calling. Your children are a gift from our Creator. How does this change the way you see your kids? How can this change the way you pray for them and parent them?

Additional Reading:

-Psalm 127:3-5, III John 1:4, Genesis 1:28
-Deuteronomy 11:19, James 1:17, Titus 2:3-5
-Mark 9:37, Proverbs 17:6, Proverbs 22:6
-Psalm 139:13-16, Matthew 18:1-6
-2 Timothy 3:15, Lamentations 3:22-23, Romans 11:29

# Sarah

"God never made a promise that was too
good to be true."
-D.L. Moody

I DON'T KNOW if there's a "Not Quite
SuperMom" in the Bible that is easier to relate
to than Sarah. I mean, she's all of us, isn't she?
Think about it: God promised her husband
that he'd have more descendants than the
stars in the sky. Abraham surely told Sarah
God's promise, and Sarah must have gone
into "GO MODE." At least, in her own mind.
Read Genesis 13:14-18 and Genesis 18:10-15.
Then read Genesis 21:1-7.

Confession time: I have been guilty of
submitting resumes on my husband's behalf.
Not that he's incapable or unwilling, but I'm
the administrative one in our family. Details
are "my thing." He's convinced I applied for

the job he has now (for him, of course.) I do not recall doing such a thing but I freely admit that I wrote his cover letter for a former position that he held (and loved, I might add.) When I know God has impressed something on my husband's heart, I'm in a hurry to see it accomplished. We call Sarah impatient. Perhaps rightly so...but I see her as a go-getter. Obviously, her method was inexcusable, and in the end, it caused a great deal of grief, but the heart behind it was at least understandable.

We should note that <u>our methods for making God's plans happen are never as good as God's way</u>. And they usually backfire. Take a minute to read Genesis 21:9-10. Ishmael was the direct fruit of Sarah's attempt to bring about God's promise. But watch her roar like a Mama Bear when Ishmael makes fun of her baby! And again, I can relate. I can't stand a bully, and I don't know a mom who is going to sit back and say nothing while her child is bullied. Regardless....Sarah, this "bully" was your idea!

> God won't change His mind about you.

You know, in all of our good intentions and best efforts to make God's will happen (and NOW), we can miss out on the miracle that takes place as He increases our faith for the journey. Instead of focusing on growing in her faith, she was focused on trying to grow the baby. When her best efforts failed, she sought a "substitute promise." She offered a Plan B. We do that too, don't we? *"Okay, I know this is what God wants, but just in case He doesn't come through when I need Him to, I'll get ready and execute the backup plan."* Only God is not a God of backup plans! He means what He says! And He can be trusted to see it through to the end!

And poor Sarah laughed. I've heard many lessons about taking God seriously, and I get it. But Sarah was an elderly woman by this time, and she was worn out.  It's like realizing your child needs an outfit washed for tomorrow and it's midnight already. Multiplied by a hundred years. She was old. And tired. (*By the way, a decade of trying to fix what God doesn't need you to fix is exhausting*.) But who of us can cast the first stone at Sarah? Not me. Yet here's the thing: for all her striving and fixing and Plan B's and inappropriate laughter, <u>GOD DID NOT CHANGE HIS MIND ABOUT SARAH</u>. He didn't give up on her. Or her old-woman womb. And God isn't giving up on you! Rest. Stop trying to make His promise happen. Let Him grow your faith. Trust. Pray. Get in the Word. And laugh with joy when the promise is fulfilled!

Reflections:

What promises are you holding onto for your life or for your children?  We live in a culture of instant gratification, but faith isn't faith when it isn't tried by time.  That's not to say that God can't come through on a promise immediately after you decide to walk in faith for it. It's just to say that He does not operate on our calendars and weekly planners. He thinks of things we could never dream about. Let Him increase your faith for this promise-journey you're on. Ask Him for help to see things from His perspective, and watch for His hand working in your life in the meantime.

When was the last time you laughed at someone's ludicrous suggestion about you? As of the writing of this book, my answer is 3 weeks ago to the day. You know what that suggestion was? That I should write a book. I know, I know. I didn't even have the tiniest idea of what I could ever write a whole book about. My answer to that crazy suggestion was laughter as I exclaimed that I am "just a podcaster, just a blogger." The sweet woman who suggested I write a book retorted: "Just! JUST! How in the world does one start a podcast? You are not JUST a podcaster or blogger." Wow. What did our moms tell us? "Never say never"? Whatever it might be that you would laugh off as completely absurd, take a moment right now to let your heart consider it. Just for a minute. You never know. Three weeks from now, it could be reality. Hold on tight, Momma! Sarah gave birth in a geriatric ward!

Additional Reading:

    -Genesis 21:6-7, Isaiah 41:10, Exodus 14:14
  -Isaiah 41:13, Isaiah 54:10, Jeremiah 29:11
  -Joshua 1:9, Romans 8:28, Psalm 9:9-10
  -Philippians 4:6-7, Proverbs 3:5-6,
Matthew 7:9-11
  -Psalm 103:2-5, John 14:13-16

# Jochebed

"Faith's most severe tests come not when we see nothing, but when we see a stunning array of evidence that seems to prove our faith vain."
-Elisabeth Elliot

THIS SUPERMOM'S ONE act of faith reverberated through the halls of history and landed her right in the famous lineup of heroes of the faith in Hebrews 11. Read verse 23 of that famous chapter.

Jochebed was Moses's mother, and, like most of us, she would have rather died than let her sweet little baby boy be slaughtered by the government ruler, Pharaoh. So she hid him as long as she could, and then she thought of a plan. Read Exodus 2: 1-10.

It's interesting to note that, in an era when God sometimes audibly told His people what to do, Jochebed didn't seem to hear from God exactly what to do. At least, we don't see that explicitly in scripture. It's almost as if her mothering instinct took over. She didn't need to wait for God to speak to her about this. Sometimes, deep down, we know instinctively what to do, or what television show to block, or what friend is negatively influencing our children. We don't need to wait for God to direct—He trusts us! Think about it: He made us mothers, and instilled in us some basic protection mechanisms that we can use to shield our children. Obviously, not every problem is so "cut and dry," and not every issue is a matter of life or death. Please don't get me wrong: we need His help and direction every single day, and He longs to be the Rock we run to when we don't know what to do about our kids. But in some cases, we can wait around on His leading when really, we're just procrastinating in dealing with something that might be difficult to enforce or carry out.

Jochebed didn't wait to hear from God about saving her son. She put him in a basket in the water where Pharaoh's daughter bathed. As the story unfolds, Moses was found, and adopted by royalty. She certainly watched him grow up from afar, but Moses later became THE leader God's people needed to be led out of the slavery of the Egyptians. God did hundreds of miracles because of the faith of Moses.

But that seed of faith was planted in his life because of a mother who was not afraid to defy the most powerful person in the world. That was *crazy* faith! And consider this: she had no idea how it would turn out. As was mentioned before, God didn't direct her or promise her anything (at least, not that we can find in scripture.) She had <u>no proof</u> that her plan would work. For all she knew, Moses could be found and killed immediately. Or, she could be caught trying to hide her baby boy. She almost certainly would have been killed. We have the benefit of hindsight: it all worked out in the end. (*Deep sigh of relief!*) Jochebed didn't get to raise her precious boy longer than a few years, but that's all it took. She made the best use of the time she did have. Moses knew who he was, even after he left Jochebed's arms: not the adopted son of a Princess, but a child of the Living God. And later, when it mattered most, he didn't forget.

Proper identity is vital for a Christian. We have to know who we are and Whose we are, especially in a world that is constantly telling our children that they can be "whoever they want to be." That's not to say that we can't encourage our children to do great things and be successful people. Instead, it means we must nurture them as young disciples, hiding God's Word in their hearts, and affirming them as warriors for Christ.

> As moms, we have the charge to instill in our children their God-given identities: sons and daughters of the King!

Jochebed's example proves that as moms, we have the charge to instill in our children their God-given identities: sons and daughters of the King, future history-makers who walk with God!

Reflections:

Is there some issue you know God would have you deal with regarding yourself or your children? Maybe it's something you know instinctively, but you have been putting it off, hoping God will outline the exact steps you should take? Ask Him to help you see how to avoid procrastinating—and how to effectively handle the situation with wisdom.

When was the last time you prayed over your children, asking God to show you their identities in Him? My son is strong, rarely emotional, and unwaveringly confident. He isn't a people-pleaser, and in the past, his heart was hard toward authority. I prayed for almost a year, asking God to take out his stony heart and give him a soft heart. (Ezekiel 36:26) God answered my prayers in big ways! And now, several years later, I know my son will be a leader for Christ. He will not care what others think; he'll lead with strength and discernment, living to please his Savior. My daughter is soft, intuitive, and full of imagination. She loves to worship, and even though she's young, she truly desires to hear from God. She asks me a thousand questions about Him, and one day I was exasperated with her wildly imaginative inquiries. I started to reprimand her, but in my heart I felt God stop me. It was as if He said, *"I love her imagination about Me. Someday, that will turn into great faith."* As she grows, I know she will worship Him with all of her heart, standing firm in her strong faith, ready to do anything He asks of her.

What seeds of faith can you plant in your children's lives? Maybe it's evening prayer time, or faith-building conversations around the dinner table—whatever it is for you, start today. Don't fret over lost time. Start now. Use the time you have with your children to pour into them God's plan and purpose for their lives!

Additional Reading:

    -John 1:12, Jeremiah 1:5, 1 Peter 2:9
    -I John 3:1-2, Isaiah 61:1-2
    -Exodus 4:10-12, Hebrews 13:20-21
    -Psalm 119:30, Matthew 17:20, Romans 15:13
    -Jeremiah 1:9, Luke 1:45, Ephesians 3:14-21

# Hannah

"Prayer is the portal that brings the power of heaven down to earth. It is kryptonite to the enemy and to all his ploys against you." - Priscilla Shirer, *Fervent*

THE BOOK OF 1 Samuel begins with the story of a Not Quite SuperMom named Hannah. In fact, to begin with, she wasn't even a mom at all. I have personally seen the heartbreak caused by infertility, and although our culture doesn't scorn barren women like Hannah's culture may have, it certainly isn't always compassionate toward the soul-affliction that it is. Read through 1 Samuel 1 and try to imagine yourself as Hannah.

Hannah was dearly loved by her husband, in spite of the ridicule she endured from his other, fertile wife, Peninnah. The Bible says that it took years of desperation, but Hannah decided to get into the presence of God for herself and plead to Him for a child. At that time, the presence of God could be found only at the temple. Today, however, for the Christ-follower, His presence can be found wherever we are. Stop for a moment and consider that.

**We are able, should we choose, to be in His presence every moment of every day.**

Hannah made a vow to God: if He'd give her a son, she'd give him back to the Lord. She was done striving for the promise through her own efforts. She was done with her selfish ambitions. She was done trying to keep up with her rival, Peninnah. She. Was. Done. She prayed like I've prayed many times: silently, with tears streaming down my face, begging God to move on my behalf. She stayed there, in that posture, for longer than was socially acceptable. The Bible says that Eli, the priest, reprimanded her and called her a drunk! Nothing like kickin' a girl when she's down. (Thanks for that, Eli. You were *awesome*.) But Hannah wasn't deterred. She explained that she'd been in prayer—deep, anguished prayer. Read Eli's response again in verse 17. Did Eli know her request? I can imagine that nearly everyone who knew Hannah knew her plight. Some burdens are visible, and some are unseen. But even the most visible burdens go deeper than what meets the eye. Fortunately, God dwells beyond just the physical realm and heals the emotional and spiritual wounds that human eyes cannot see. Hannah's heart cry for a baby was more than a physical need; read 1 Samuel 1:16. Hers was a prayer that may have started out of a feeling of resentment. It would not be a hard stretch to imagine that the reason she took so long to go to the temple to pour her heart out was that she was blaming God. He created our bodies, and her body was not able to carry a baby the way God originally intended.

Although I have seen the heartbreak it causes, I don't have personal experience with infertility. But I have spent years

> Our lack of belief in a truth does not invalidate that truth.

thinking that God made a mistake when He created my body. I remember a day I read Psalm 139:14 with a fresh perspective. I realized that I needed to thank God for the way He had made me, in spite of how I felt. I wasn't "there" yet. But I thanked Him anyway. In some ways, I'm still not "there" yet. But our lack of belief in a truth does not invalidate that truth. Let me say it another way: if God says that you are wonderful, beautiful in His sight (and He does!), your inability to see that doesn't make it untrue! Hannah had to lay down her resentment against God and His creation of her body. That was a vital part of her surrender.

When was the last time you entered into His presence with such profound desperation that you didn't care what anyone thought of how long you lingered at the altar or in your place of prayer? We all have needs so great that we can hardly speak the words out loud. A powerful shift takes place when we enter in to His presence and lay it all down at His feet. Faith grows. Perspective changes. God's heart is touched with our grief. And we never leave that place the same. Hannah's faith grew. It was obvious because even before she saw the promise fulfilled, the Bible says that she left there, able to eat, and no longer looking despondent. Let Him change your vision, Momma. Get in His presence today and don't leave until something changes. You may not see it completed immediately, but your eyes of faith will see what you could never see before.

Reflections:

Think back on times when you know you have been in the presence of God. Consider the atmosphere. Was it always the same? Did it change by location? How can we spend time in His presence all the time? How can we walk in it constantly? For me, and maybe for most moms, quiet places aren't always possible. I try to utilize them whenever I can! But being in His presence daily means keeping an open dialogue with Him all day, every day. I'm not always successful (kids can be loud and distracting!), but there is an obvious difference in my day when I am prioritizing my prayer conversation with Him. Worship music helps as well. The atmosphere of bickering and strife between my kids often eases with good music in the background. My stress level plummets, and my heart is focused on Him. Try it for yourself. He's patient, and He'll help you get there.

Additional Reading:

-Psalm 139:7-8, Jeremiah 29:13, I Kings 8:27
-Psalm 113:9, Mark 11:24, Romans 12:12
-Psalm 127:3, Luke 1:36-37
-Isaiah 54:1-17
-Psalm 147:3, Psalm 128:3, Psalm 139:16

# Lois

"Where there is a grandmother in the house the children always have a friend." -Swedish Proverb

GRANDMOTHERS HAVE A unique role in the lives of their grandchildren, don't they? As of last August, both of my grandmas have passed away. It's safe to say I was heartbroken both times. Their love feels different, doesn't it?  Lois, Timothy's grandmother, was the only woman referred to in the Bible as a "grandmother." According to the *Strong's Concordance*, the Greek word for "grandmother" was *mamme*, and pronounced "mammy."  I adore this little tidbit; she wasn't just Timothy's grandma, she was his "Mammy." She was not only a SuperMom--according to Paul, she was a Super-Grandma of the faith! Read 2 Timothy 1:5 and Psalm 103:17.

Lois was only mentioned by name once in the Bible, but her life had eternal impact. Sometimes it's not about who you are, but who you influence. She was a godly influence in Timothy's life, and if you know anything about Timothy, you know he worked right alongside Paul in reaching his world for Christ. And Lois had a part in every soul that was won through Timothy's ministry. Lois was known for her "unfeigned" faith, and that's what she imparted to her grandson, Timothy. According to *Merriam-Webster's collegiate dictionary*, that word, *unfeigned*, means genuine, not hypocritical.

Her faith didn't waver when she left the church building. She didn't praise God on Sundays and curse her neighbor on Monday morning. It was real to her, and Timothy watched her live it out. Nevertheless, Timothy wasn't <u>forced</u> to follow in the faith of his grandmother; every child and grandchild has a free will. Still, the choice to follow Christ was likely made easier for him because it was so real to her. When I was a kid, my pastor, Pastor David Garnett, used to say, "Never underestimate the power of a praying grandmother." I've seen it over and over:

> Godly mothers and grandmothers influence ENTIRE generations.

godly grandmas influence generations. Maybe you're like me, far from being a grandma. It's never too early to start praying for our future grandchildren and living out a genuine faith for our own children to see. And in the meantime, we can love and encourage our kids' grandmothers, reminding our children that their grandmas have wisdom and love to share that will last long after they've grown

up. There's a word for it: *legacy*. It smells like a
well-worn Bible and tastes like homemade
cookies.

Reflections:

Do you have a grandparent or older relative
that influenced you spiritually? What did that
look like?

What are some practical things we can do
now to establish a legacy of faith for our
children and grandchildren?

Additional Reading:

   -Job 5:25, Isaiah 44:3, Proverbs 17:6
   -Isaiah 46:4-5, Psalm 37:25
   -Proverbs 16:31, Psalm 103:7, Titus 2:3
   -Psalm 90:12, Isaiah 40:28-32
   -Deuteronomy 4:9, 5:16 Psalm 145:4

# Eunice

"Only God Himself fully appreciates the
influence of a Christian mother in the molding
of character in her children."
-Billy Graham

EUNICE IS RIGHT in the middle of a list of
amazing pillars of faith in 2 Timothy 1:5, but I
believe she deserves her own "Not Quite
SuperMom" status.  Read Proverbs 22: 6 and
Deuteronomy 11:19-28.
   There are things we can deduce about
Eunice's life in between the lines of scripture.
Eunice was Lois's daughter and Timothy's
mother. Lois is heralded as a Godly
grandmother, and rightly so. But we'd be
wrong to overlook the momma in the middle.
She's characterized as having the same
"unfeigned" faith as Lois. A godly
grandmother may influence her grandchildren
mightily, but her hands can be tied if there
isn't a parent willing to support and reinforce
that influence. Eunice had just as great a role

as Lois did in planting the seeds of faith in young Timothy's heart!

Read Acts 16:1-3. Timothy's father was likely not a Christian. Raising Timothy to live for Christ without the support from her husband could not have been an easy task. Raising children to love Jesus is difficult, no matter the circumstances. But raising a godly son when you are the only parent trying to do so must have been nothing short of grueling. The one verse in which she's named indicates that she didn't waver, never gave up. She hid God's Word in her little boy's heart and he didn't forget it.  You can see the proof in 2 Timothy 3:15.

> Sometimes it's not about who you are, but whom you influence.

You may not have a ton of support, Momma. You may feel completely alone trying to raise your kids to serve Jesus. But take heart! Your Heavenly Father said He will never leave you or forsake you. Keep your eyes fixed on Him. He's walking with you every step of the way, on the good days and on the really tough days when you want to give up. Be firm and faithful, and watch God do miracles in your children's lives.

Reflections:

Single moms probably feel a lot like Eunice felt trying to raise Timothy.  Even though she had a husband, his lack of faith likely made her feel alone—except for Lois, of course. Are you a single mom? Or a married mom whose husband doesn't know Christ? The Bible says that your testimony of faith can win your husband to the Lord. If you're a single momma, next Sunday at church, look around you and find yourself a "Lois." She might not be a blood relative of yours, but a woman of unwavering faith will not mind your asking for some support. Nearly every church I've attended has at least one "Lois" in the congregation. Her name might be "Carol" or "Joan," but she's got more than enough wisdom and love to share, and I bet she'll be happy to help support you on your mothering journey. Take the step. Ask her. If you're a mom, married to a believing husband, look around you at church next Sunday. Can you spot a "Eunice"? You may not have years of wisdom to offer, but you might have an extra few spots at your dining room table for an occasional meal. Or maybe you can keep her children for a few hours to help give her a break? Find a way to support the mommas around you who are struggling.

Additional Reading:

    -2 Corinthians 1:3-4, Proverbs 14:1
    -James 1:2-4, Matthew 11:28-30
    -I John 5:14-15, Psalm 73:25-26
    -Psalm 13:5-6, Hebrews 10:24-25
    -Jeremiah 17:7-8, Habakkuk 3:19

# Rebekah

"Our goal in parenting is not ultimately for our
kids to get a great education or be great
atheletes or to find a great husband or get a
great career. Our goal is for them to love a
great God."
-David Platt

REBEKAH WAS ONE of those Not Quite
SuperMoms in the Bible that we're quick to
disassociate from. As moms, we look back at
her story and say to ourselves, *"I'm nothing
like her."* Phew. Dodged *that* bullet.

But her story isn't in the Bible to make us
feel like better moms. It's an example. Maybe
it's a warning of sorts. If we'll be honest,
there's a tiny bit of Rebekah in all of us, and, if
we aren't careful, there can be a whole lot of
Rebekah in any of us.

Read Genesis 24. It all started out good.
Like Eve, she was an answer to Isaac's need
for a wife. Abraham's servant was sent to
"fetch" a wife for Issac. Without Isaac. Sight
unseen. I can imagine the heavenly audience
sitting on the edge of their seats as Rebekah

was asked, "Will you go with the servant [to marry the man you've never met]?" And the deep sigh of relief as she responded, "I will go." Rebekah and Isaac were a match made in heaven, quite literally. Their story rivals some of the best Hollywood has ever offered.

But 20 years later, when Rebekah became pregnant with twin boys, things started to shift. Children can reveal "blind spots" in even the best marriages and the strongest faith. We're often quick to see the blind spots in other parents' lives. Jesus warned us in Matthew 7:3-5 about blind spots, and we're wrong if we think we're somehow above the sort of blind spots that Isaac and Rebekah had.

Genesis 25:28 says it plainly: Isaac favored one twin, Esau, and Rebekah favored the other, Jacob. Isaac was definitely not blameless in this SuperMom account, but we'll have to save his story for a "SuperDads" book.  Strong marriage, right? Favoritism? Really? These are the reasons why it's so easy to disassociate ourselves from her story. Surely we would never play favorites with *our* kids.

But stay with me for a second: Rebekah had a blind spot. She wanted her son Jacob to succeed in life AT ALL COSTS. In the end, she went so far as to help and encourage Jacob to deceive his father, Isaac! As a result, her life was never the same, and her beloved son had to run for his life from his angry brother Esau. All this came about because of Rebekah wanting her favorite son to have his father's financial and spiritual blessing.

There's nothing wrong with wanting our kids to succeed in life. Rebekah's desire to see her son prosper wasn't necessarily the blind spot. It became a blind spot for her when she was willing to convince Jacob to deceive others in order to "win" the prize. When we neglect what we know is right in order to get ahead, we've either knowingly or unknowingly entered a blind area. That distinction--whether or not she knew (or we know)--what's happening, is not really mine to make. All I'll say is this: the enemy is subtle. He'll use shiny gold medals and prestigious awards to lure us (and our children) into compromise.

The problem with blind spots is that we don't realize they're there. It's unlikely that Rebekah knew she'd go down in history as the mom who favored one son above his twin brother. It's dangerous to think we have no blind spots when it comes to our kids. So what can we do?

> The problem with blind spots in parenting is that we don't know they're there. But the Holy Spirit is ready to reveal them to us if we ask Him to.

We've got to get to know our Father's heart for our kids. Ask the Holy Spirit to reveal what you're missing--to give you spiritual eyes to see the blind spots in your life. They may have nothing to do with your kids. He can and will reveal them to you and help you see how to go forward. All you have to do is ask. But I'll leave you with this sincere warning: before you ask the Holy Spirit to reveal the areas you aren't seeing clearly, make certain you're ready to surrender, regardless of His answer. Because if you're not ready to begin the process of correcting those areas, you run the risk of slipping into full rebellion and a quenching of the Holy Spirit. Don't stay intentionally blind, Momma. Seek freedom. Embrace it. And let Him help you finally see your blind spots with His eyes.

Reflections:

When was the last time you were faced with a moment of clarity to realize that you had been living with a blind spot? How did the Holy Spirit help you then?

If you're like me, you hope you aren't missing anything when it comes to your kids. We all know parents who think their child can do no wrong. It may seem obvious to us, but that mom and dad may be oblivious. Is it possible that I'm oblivious to some glaring issue in my own family? Jesus said to beware. Don't be so quick to point out that other mom's blind spot. Spend a moment writing out a prayer of surrender, asking the Holy Spirit to show you those areas in your own life; not so you can justifiably point out that other mom's "speck," but rather so that you will experience

complete freedom and healing in your own
home.  Ask Him now.


Additional Reading:

   -Ephesians 6:4, Psalm 78:4, I Chronicles 28:9
   -Psalm 103:13, Proverbs 13:24, Colossians 3:16
   -Psalm 139:23-24, Jeremiah 17:9-10
   -Proverbs 21:2, Psalm 19:12-14
   -Romans 2:1-3, Galatians 5:22-23

# Lot's Wife

"If you look at the world, you'll be distressed. If you look within, you'll be depressed. But if you look at Christ, you'll be at rest."
-Corrie Ten Boom

READ GENESIS 19. Talk about an example. Honestly, ever since I was a kid and visited Washington, D.C., I always picture Lot's wife as one of the monuments in our capitol, standing there for generations as a memorial. The harsh reality is that this Not Quite SuperMom disobeyed God's explicit command (given through His angels) and was turned into a pillar of salt for her disobedience. He told them not to look back at their burning city. She looked back, bottom line. And she became an actual physical monument, reminding her descendants that God means what He says.

And then there's us.

I, for one, am so glad God doesn't deal with us the way He dealt with people in the Old Testament. Just yesterday, I could've been turned into a pillar of salt at least 3 times.

Why?

Because I looked back.

See, even though we aren't asked to leave a wretched, burning city like Lot's wife was, the New Testament mandate to "leave behind" is found in Philippians 3:3. Then in Hebrews 12:1, we are told to lay aside the sin that so easily bogs us down. We're supposed to look to Jesus.

Not our past.

Not the yelling match we had with our kids yesterday.

Not our failure to get in the Word at all last week... Or last month... Or last year.

Not the arguments we had with our husbands this morning.

Not the shortcomings or the missteps or the days without prayer or worship or even acknowledgment of God at all.

<u>We aren't supposed to look back.</u>

I hear you thinking, *"But sometimes it's good to look back, right? All the blessings God has given us, and all the amazing miracles He's done...."* And you're right. Some have used the illustration of the rearview mirror: if you drove with your eyes only on what's behind you, you'd crash. But reflection can be helpful if you're looking at the *blessings* of your past, not the *failures*. And, as a side note, if you live in constant

> If you live in constant reflection on what God USED to do in your life, chances are you may be missing what He's trying to do in the here and now.

reflection on what God used to do in your life, chances are you may be missing what He's trying to do in the here and now. Keep your eyes on Him today. And tomorrow. And the next day. And, if you're like me, and you sneak a peek at your past failures, confess it quickly. Let Him gently nudge your chin back around so your eyes meet His and your focus is fixed on His prize--your calling, and the amazing future He has planned for you.

Reflections:

What thought might have triggered Lot's wife to turn around--her beloved home in flames? Her whole life turning to ash behind her? What thoughts trigger your flashbacks of past failures?

Instead of dwelling on our regrets and mistakes, what are some practical things we can do to stay forward focused?

Additional Reading:

   -Hebrews 12:2, Jeremiah 29:13, Isaiah 26:3
   -Jeremiah 24:7, Psalm 57:7, Colossians 3:1
   -Philippians 3:13-14, Psalm 123:2
   -Psalm 91:14-15, Psalm 112:7, Psalm 46:10
   -Psalm 16:8, II Corinthians 4:18, Hebrews 3:1

# Elizabeth

"Worship is our response...to God for Who He is, and what He has done; expressed in and by the things we say and the way we live."
-Louie Giglio

THIS NOT QUITE SuperMom was the mother of John the Baptist, who was prophesied in Isaiah 40:3. He's best known for setting the stage for the Messiah. He never brought attention to himself: he pointed everyone to Jesus. *But he learned it from his mom.* Read Luke 1.

Elizabeth had been unable to conceive, just like Sarah and Hannah centuries before. She had likely given up hope of ever having a child, and the Bible does not record anything about her life prior to Luke 1. But after the angel Gabriel appeared to her husband, Zechariah, to announce the upcoming birth of a son, Elizabeth became pregnant! What an exciting miracle! I can picture her, amazed, maybe even shocked. She probably ran to tell her friends as fast as she could. If there had been Facebook, she might have posted a "teaser" status: "Anyone have diaper coupons? *Wink*"

A while later, her cousin Mary came to visit. Mary, the engaged--but unwed--mother. Elizabeth could have reacted so many ways; she could have shut the door in Mary's face. *How dare she come waddling over with her young, glowing face?* Especially after Elizabeth had waited so long-- as a married woman, no less--for her own precious pregnancy! Or, she could have been the "older, wiser, more spiritual" cousin who could counsel Mary about her sinful ways. Both reactions would have been completely natural. We are often quick to cast judgment on a mom's situation by everything we can see, you know? But Elizabeth didn't react **naturally**. She responded **supernaturally**. She was tuned in to the Holy Spirit, and she KNEW that her baby jumped nearly out of her belly because Mary's pregnancy was SUPERNATURAL. She immediately pointed to her Savior, and we can easily imagine that she raised her son to do the same. Read Elizabeth's response in Luke 1:43-45.

> Sometimes we react naturally when we should be reacting supernaturally.

As humans, we naturally lean toward self-promotion. It's against human nature to point the limelight toward another. But isn't that the Gospel—lifting up Christ and pointing souls to Him? Jesus gave His life on a cross for sins of the entire world. And He said if He is lifted up, He'll draw all people to Himself. Just as the SuperMom Elizabeth did, we are called to point our children to their Savior. His promise is true today: if we lift Him up, He'll draw our kids in too. Tell them how good He is and how much He loves them. Tell them how He died for them. Sing His praises, literally. Lift Him up. And watch for the supernatural to take place in their hearts as they come to know the Savior you worship.

Reflections:

"Lifting Jesus up" sounds theoretical to me. What are some practical ways you can lift Him up to your kids? For me, I think I don't share enough about what God is doing in my own heart. I can do better sharing testimonies and personal victories He's given me.

How can we do better with taking younger women under our wings? Elizabeth hid Mary for several months during a time when others would have certainly judged her situation negatively. How can we help those moms around us who may be inwardly struggling?

Additional Reading:

-Psalm 115:4-8. John 12:32
-John 6:44-45, Colossians 1:19-20
-Ephesians 1:10, Romans 10:13-14
-I Chronicles 16:23-31
-Psalm 29

# Abigail

"This is the secret to finding and keeping lasting friendships: become women who want to see the women around them flourish."
-Lisa-Jo Baker, *Never Unfriended*

FOR NOW, LET'S call this SuperMom a "Not Quite Superwoman." Like some others we've highlighted, she wasn't a mom when her story began. Read 1 Samuel 25.

Humor me while I describe Abigail in a "modern" setting: she's got a college education. Her hair is perfectly styled and her roots never show. She's fit, hitting the home gym every morning without fail. Her Bible is well-worn, and her prayer journal is opened daily. Her home is decorated like the pages of a magazine, and her weekly shopping trips include stops at all the best boutiques. Her personal cook and housekeeper adore her, and her Instagram account has 450k followers. You might know her. Or, you might follow her Instagram account. You might secretly wish you could be her. I can't blame you. I would want to be her too! But beyond those pristine photo filters, her marriage is a mess. Her husband is a drunken, incorrigible man, and she silently wipes tears as she "fixes" his messes. She is a peacemaker on his behalf, carrying the weight of the world on her shoulders day after day.

I know, I know. The Bible doesn't say all that about Abigail, but it DOES say that she was wise, and peacekeeping, and wealthy (at least, her husband was.) It also mentions that she was pretty. In today's world, she could have been everything described above.

> Instagram filters can hide a host of heartache. Don't assume another momma isn't struggling just because her social media looks good.

However, her home life was miserable, to put it mildly. The Bible describes Nabal, her husband, as a cruel and brutal man in all his dealings. And yet, despite being married to such a man, she didn't waver in her faithfulness to her loathsome husband.

The story takes an unexpected turn when the future king, David, came along. Her husband was rude to David and his men, and David planned retaliation. Abigail secretly defied her husband and humbly approached David with food and an offer of peace, taking the blame for her husband. Sadly, she'd probably had to do this many times before.

I love how Abigail wisely approaches David —first with food, and then with reason. There's very little that a good meal can't pacify! In addition to the food offering, she humbly suggested to David that to avenge himself by killing her husband (as well as their entire household—including Abigail herself) would not be in his best interests. She de-escalated the situation by appealing to his conscience; she reminded him of who he was: the Lord's soldier, fighting *His* battles. She gently suggested that he would later regret having this bloodshed on his hands, and she prophesied that all of his enemies would be as cursed as her husband was. Talk about a crisis negotiator! I need some of that wisdom in refereeing my kids' bickering! (Side note: when in doubt, feed them.)

Since you already read 1 Samuel 25, you know the crazy twist at the end of the story: Nabal died immediately, Abigail married David a short time later, and she eventually became the mother of David's son, Daniel. The bottom line is, I don't have a clue what struggles you're facing based on your social media posts. I can imagine that those pretty filters hide a lot of tears. You don't know what another mom is facing either. Don't wish for her life, no matter how good it looks. Instead, we need to pray for each other. Call a friend today and ask if there's anything you can pray about. It may look like she's got it all together, but she may be silently begging God for a friend. Be that one. And if you're the one struggling behind closed doors, <u>reach out</u>. Ask your Father to bring you a trusted confidant who may be able to give you wise, godly counsel.

Reflections:

When was the last time you secretly wished for another mom's life? Even if you didn't say it out loud, or let the thought fully form—was it today?

In what areas are you most likely to covet what another mom has? Have you considered that those areas may be places God wants to heal in your own life? For instance, if you constantly struggle to be content with the way your house looks, have you considered that you may need God's healing in feeling insecure? Or maybe it's about your body shape or your hair texture--Your heavenly Father longs to touch those areas in your life. Let Him!

Think of a friend who seems to have it all together. Stop right now and pray for that woman. We all have unseen needs. You may not know what hers are, but pray for her anyway. She may be putting out fires you know nothing about.

Additional Reading:

-II Corinthians 10:12, Galatians 1:10,
Philippians 2:3
-II Timothy 2:15, Galatians 6:4, Hebrews 12:1
-I John 2:15, Matthew 6:33-34
-I Timothy 6:6-7, Ezekiel 16:13-14
-Song of Solomon 2:16, Proverbs 31:10-31

# Naomi

"Only you can decide how your fires will affect you.  Will you be sanctified or scarred?"
-Beth Moore, *A Woman's Heart*

THIS NOT QUITE SuperMom experienced a level of grief that is almost unrivaled anywhere else in Scripture, except, perhaps, in the story of Job. Read Ruth 1. She and her husband and their two boys left the Promised Land in search of a better life.  There was famine in Judah, and the land of Moab promised food. So they left and went to Moab. And then, the unthinkable: her husband passed away and left her a single mother to their two sons, in a foreign, godless land. The sons eventually married, but tragedy didn't let up; 10 years later, they both died. Can you imagine?! Her table, once full of laughter around family dinners, was now empty and grief-stricken, with only her two daughters-in-law left to grieve along with her.

As the story goes, the three women left Moab to return to Naomi's homeland, because word had spread that the famine there was over. I can picture Naomi thinking as they traveled, perhaps reliving in her mind's eye her initial journey to Moab with a caravan full of her two rambunctious boys, her big, strapping husband, and bushels of hope. But then maybe she stopped abruptly, looking at the grieving young widows traveling with her. She herself had been widowed for years. She knew the pain and heartbreak all too well. Heaven forbid they live with that cloud of sorrow over them too! Her only solution was to send them back to their own parents, to the lives they'd known before, in hopes that they'd remarry there and find a new life, leaving behind the sadness and pain of loss. But Ruth wouldn't go. She stayed with Naomi and promised never to leave her. Read Ruth 2.

When they arrived, people barely recognized the woman she once was. But Naomi insisted that her old friends call her a new name, "Mara." *Bitter*. Naomi felt alone, in spite of Ruth's presence. She felt neglected by the God she once knew.

She had taken on a new identity--a sad, empty identity—one without God's presence. It was a life full of suffering and grief with no end in sight.

Naomi's story is a heartbreaking reminder that we can never be satisfied beyond Jesus. His is the only love that fills all of the voids in us. When we try to fill a need outside of Him, it only leaves us bitter, sad, and forgetting who we really are.

It's probably not as dramatic a departure

as Naomi's—yours and mine.    We don't
usually pack up our lives and leave town to
chase what we hope will satisfy. Instead, it's
the little things in little ways--distractions that
turn our hearts away from His. If you're in a
season of feeling low, or somehow not
yourself, look around you. Have you let your
focus slip? Have you filled your life with
busyness and stress and doing and lost the
purpose of it all?  It happens so quickly--we
can miss the signs.  It
looks innocent at first.
But before long, we've
grown bitter, far from
the close relationship
we once enjoyed with
our Abba Father.  But

> All it takes for
> reconciliation is a
> bended knee and a
> repentant heart.

there's good news! All it takes for
reconciliation is a bended knee and a
repentant heart. He'll restore your joy and
identity in one fell swoop and welcome you
back into His outstretched arms.

Reflections:

Do you remember a time when you realized
you had lost your focus and started to fill your
life with things that weren't satisfying?  What
did that look like? What did it feel like?

It's so easy to let our focus slip.  What are
some practical ways you can remind yourself
to find your joy and satisfaction in His
presence?  For me, it's a matter of setting the
atmosphere in my home and in my life. Most

days, that looks like worship music on in the background of whatever I'm doing, prioritizing my quiet time, and keeping a constant prayer dialogue going with my Father. I can't stress it enough, however; it takes very little to distract my heart. A day or two of being really busy can easily leave me feeling like I'm "not myself." Don't let it creep in, Momma. Fight it like your life depends on it.

Additional Reading:

-Psalm 16:11, Psalm 3:3, Revelation 21:4
-Psalm 34:18, Psalm 73:26, Psalm 147:3
-Isaiah 53:4-6, Joshua 1:9
-Matthew 5:4, II Corinthians 1:3-4
-Isaiah 41:10, Psalm 23:4, I Thessalonians 4:13-14

# Ruth

> "God is able to take the mess of our past and turn it into a message. He takes the trials and tests and turns them into a testimony."
> -Christine Caine, *Undaunted*

RUTH WAS A SuperMom who needed a Redeemer. If that's all I knew about Ruth, I could already relate to her. I don't know about you, but I need someone to rescue me from myself most days! And what a Redeemer He is: He rescues me every day!!!!

The story of Ruth began with the story of Naomi. You can't have one without the other. Make sure you've read about Naomi before you begin this study of Ruth. Then read Ruth 2 and this time, put yourself in Ruth's sandals.

There's something nagging my heart about the relationship between Naomi and Ruth. Ruth refused to return to her own family after Naomi insisted she do so. Ruth chose to leave behind her own people, her own religion, and everything she knew in order to follow her mother-in-law. Look at Ruth 1:16-17 again. She accepted Naomi's God as hers. She knew, somehow, that her gods would not be welcomed back in Judah. She knew the decision to stay with Naomi would mean she was accepting and believing in Naomi's God. In spite of the poor decision to leave Judah, and the years of sorrow that followed, Naomi must have demonstrated a faith that touched Ruth's heart.

Ruth became a living example of repentance. She chose to leave behind her old life—the gods she had served and even her family who had served them. She left all of that behind and in an "about-face" move, she wholeheartedly chose to serve the One True God, the One Naomi served. And she stayed true to her word.

In Judah, though, Naomi knew that Ruth needed a "kinsman-redeemer" to marry her and secure the family land they were in danger of losing. Boaz, a family relative, was that redeemer. He didn't care where Ruth was from or what she had done or what gods she had served in the past. Let me whisper this truth straight to your heart, sweet Momma: your Redeemer doesn't care either. He welcomes you into His family, just as you are. He redeems your life-- and as you begin to know Him, you'll see that He replaces your filthy rags with His righteousness. You're accepted. Beloved. Adored. Like a gorgeous,

> Your Redeemer doesn't care where you came from or what you did before you were His daughter.

glowing bride. He's chosen YOU. As you are. So look into His loving eyes, remember that you belong to Him, and go live for Him with your head held high and your heart full. You. Are. Redeemed.

Reflections:

Is there an area of your life that you haven't completely left behind yet? Are you still holding on to regrets and failures of the past? Take a moment and ask your Redeemer to help you let go completely.

Ruth was not born into a God-honoring home, yet her marriage to Boaz put her in the ancestry and lineage of Christ. Her past was not held against her after she left behind her previous life and embraced a life of following God. You have no idea what future plans God has for you, if only you'll let Him lead you out of the "old" and into the "new" you. Will you let Him today?

Additional Reading:

> -Ephesians 1:7, I Timothy 2:6, I Corinthians 6:20
> -I Peter 1:18-19, Revelation 5:9
> -Colossians 1:13-14, Isaiah 44:22
> -Galatians 4:4-7, Isaiah 52:3
> -Job 19:25, Job 33:28, John 3:16

# Deborah

"Lovely One, if you dare to dream, you must be brave enough to fight." -Lisa Bevere, *Girls with Swords*

WE DON'T ACTUALLY know if this SuperMom was a mother in the traditional sense. But God made her a mother figure over His people. Read Judges 4. Any mother who has spent a summer break at home with her children can easily imagine what it was like for Deborah to judge and referee disputes among the Israelites. Moms need the patience of Job, the wisdom of Solomon, and the bravery of Deborah every single day. (*And all the mommas said, "Amen."*)

The Bible says that she was a wife and prophetess who heard from God and offered wise counsel in leading His people. Her job description really doesn't sound much different than any Christian momma's. God told her to tell Barak to go to war against Israel's enemies. While that may have been hundreds of years ago, our kids have to fight the enemy even today. Barak, in all his "valor," refused to fight without Deborah going along with him. Our kids aren't seasoned warriors against the enemy of their souls; sometimes, they will not be willing or able to fight the enemy on their own. They're still learning to put on the whole armor of God. They need us, as parents, to lead them into spiritual battle-- until they can learn to fight on their own. Again, Ephesians 6 is the best preparation we have to help our children be ready to fight against wickedness.

The type of battles our kids face don't usually involve actual swords and shields and bad guys, but rather "harmless" video games and YouTube searches. Their battles are against bullies, or "friends" who encourage them to lie to us. It may seem less important because perhaps we aren't sending them off to fight in physical wars. But the "principalities" our children face today are greater, maybe, than in any other time period of history. Don't be deceived; Deborah's army may have faced 10,000 armed men, but our children face just as many threats or more. However, just like her army, "the Lord is marching ahead" of our kids too! It's up to us to

> Your heavenly Father trusts YOU with your kids. You're the best woman for the job!

be strong, have faith, and lead our children into victory over the enemy. Our world needs strong, God-fearing mommas who will not back down, give up, or surrender to peer pressure.

Reflections:

In what ways is God asking you to lead your children in spiritual battle? How does a leader prepare for that?

While she may not have been a mother naturally, Deborah was a spiritual mother to God's people. Do you have a spiritual mentor who is not afraid to speak truth into your life? Why is it important to seek out counsel from someone who has fought the battles we are now facing?

> Our kids aren't seasoned warriors against the enemy of their souls. They need us to lead them into battle until they can fight on their own.

Additional Reading:

- -James 4:7, II Corinthians 10:3-5
- -Isaiah 54:17, Romans 8:37, I Corinthians 15:57
- -Luke 10:19, II Thessalonians 3:3, Matthew 18:18-19
- -Deuteronomy 28:7, I Timothy 6:12, Joshua 23:10
- -Romans 8:31, Psalm 18:39, Psalm 91:1-4

# Esther

"The remarkable thing about God is that when you fear God, you fear nothing else, whereas if you do not fear God, you fear everything else."
-Oswald Chambers

ESTHER'S STORY EARNED her an entire book of the Bible. Talk about a SuperMom! She has had many books written about her life, and Beth Moore's study of Esther was one of my favorites. For a quick snapshot of her life, read Esther 2:5-20.

Esther wasn't married when her story began, but in perfect fairy tale form, she goes from being a poor orphan to becoming the queen of the land. Talk about a Royal Wedding. I don't know about you, but if I were to be propelled into a position of royalty, I would probably find it hard to focus on anything more than royal duties: shopping for the next ballgown, choosing jewels for my tiara, and scheduling spa sessions.

But Esther didn't forget who had helped raise her: her cousin, Mordecai. She didn't forget that they were Jews, God's chosen people. She didn't forget her identity when it would have been easy and convenient to do so--because her people were about to be annihilated, and Esther had never told her husband, the king, that she was a Jew.

You may be familiar with the story: Esther, in an act of unprecedented courage, went before the king to ask him to spare her and her people. He could have killed her on the spot. He could have refused her request and killed her along with all of her people. Instead, he granted her request, saving an entire nation. All because one woman wasn't afraid to speak up.

Esther later had a son, Darius II, who rebuilt the temple in Jerusalem. She may not have been a mom during that earlier, tumultuous time—but one thing is clear: she might never have had a chance to become a mom had she not stood up for her people when she had the chance. Read Esther 4:13-14.

I don't know your situation or your sphere of influence. I'm guessing that you aren't a princess or queen. *(If you are, I'd love to talk to you!)* But we all have ways of making a difference in the areas God has given us influence. If you are a stay-at-home-mom like I have been in the past, the decisions you make for your family today can

> Wherever you are, whatever your daily routine is, Momma—you are there for "such a time as this."

positively affect your children and your husband for years to come. If you're working outside the home, you are faced with daily decisions as well. Don't think for a moment that your position, wherever it may be, is insignificant. Wherever you are, whatever your daily routine is, Momma—YOU are there for such a time as this. Your life is important, and the influence you have may be life-changing. Don't discount the monotony of your daily grind. Ask God for ways to make a difference, and then, ask Him for the strength and courage to seize the opportunities as they come.

Reflections:

As moms, it's easy to fall into the routine of getting kids out the door to school, scheduling appointments, working a job, or writing grocery lists. We often focus on our to-do list for today. We rarely think about influencing nations or saving lives. But have you considered that it may be within your power to change someone's entire life? With just an encouraging word, you can enable another mom to see past the depression or discouragement that has her bound and point her to the One Who is her hope. What are some ways you can make a difference?

Additional Reading:

-Psalm 3:3, Exodus 4:15, Psalm 94:19
-Psalm 27:1, Deuteronomy 31:6, Jeremiah 29:11
-Psalm 118:6, 56:11, Hebrews 13:6
-Proverbs 29:25, Daniel 10:19
-1 Peter 2:9, 1 John 3:1-2

# The Breadmaking Widow

"I am afraid the only safe rule is to give more than we can spare." -C.S. Lewis

THIS SUPERMOM WAS never named, and her story isn't long, but it's rich with wisdom and the ingredients we need to be moms of faith. Read I Kings 17:7-16.   Can you smell the homemade bread already?

First of all, the fact that this mom was a widow indicates that she carried the entire burden of provision for herself and her son on her own shoulders.  She was determined to do her best to make sure they ate.  The pantry was empty.  The bank account was empty too. Widows and single moms are SuperMoms by default, and I can imagine that the burden she carried is a familiar one to many moms.

In spite of her own needs and burden, this widow was willing to give water to Elijah, the man of God.   Sometimes, when we are running on "empty" ourselves, we fail to notice the opportunities for kindness and hospitality that exist all around us. It's easy to do. Understandable, even. But what's "natural" can rarely yield "supernatural" results.

Now, when Elijah asked her to make the bread and give it to him, he was going a step too far, wasn't he? I mean, we are supposed to provide for our children, right? What would her son eat? I can imagine the thoughts running through her mind. I would be thinking the same thing!

But her son was likely listening in on this exchange. Elijah promised that God would provide for her and her son if she would feed the man of God first. She had a choice: faith or fear.

If she responded with fear, hoarding her meager resources, the outcome of the story might have been quite different. She was convinced that this was her final loaf of bread. She was sure they'd die from starvation after it was gone. Her fear, had she embraced it, may have resulted in her funeral.

Instead, she responded in faith. She believed God. She believed Elijah. She offered all she had left, trusting that God would provide. And although the Bible doesn't say it, I'm positive her son knew it. He probably sat there, mouth watering, while Elijah savored the bread that would have been his last meal. But then, I can imagine his mother calling out from the kitchen that she was mixing up the next batch—a miraculous

73

provision in reward for a mother's act of faith.

> Natural reasoning of conservation and hoarding never sees supernatural provision.

We have lived through seasons of lean pantries. We have never scraped the bottom of the barrel, however. I have never gathered our "last meal." My children have seen God provide for us in miraculous ways, regardless, and this widow's story challenges me to remind my children of God's constant blessing in our lives.

See, it's tempting when we have very little to turn a blind eye to the tithe envelope or the various needs for hospitality. But the natural reasoning of conservation and hoarding never sees supernatural provision. Take a step of faith, Momma. Trust God to meet your needs and give as God leads you!

Reflections:

Giving can be a huge step of faith when the numbers don't add up. Making a meal for a neighbor can be difficult when there's still a week until grocery day. Have you seen God provide miraculously in your family? Write about the miracle and make sure to share it with your children, even if it was years ago. Your faith builds theirs.

Our children see more than we sometimes realize. While I don't believe we should "burden" our children with our own financial stresses, I do believe we should include our children in our prayers for provision; on the same token, we should offer our children frequent opportunities to give to others. In what ways can you teach your children sacrificial giving? When they pray with you, they see miracles happen!

Additional Reading:

-Luke 6:38, Acts 20:35, Matthew 6:21
-2 Corinthians 9:6-7, 1 John 3:17
-Matthew 10:42, Provers 21:13, 22:9
-1 Timothy 6:18-19, John 3:16
-Galatians 6:2, Hebrews 13:16

# The Proverbs 31 Mom

"It's okay to not be perfect." -Becky Thompson

THIS MOM TAKES the title "SuperMom" to a whole other level. In just one chapter of the Bible, I find a standard of motherhood I consistently fail to achieve. Read Proverbs 31. This nameless momma puts us all to shame, doesn't she?

Forgive me while I skip over that chapter....right? But is she really as perfect as she sounds? Are you telling me she NEVER yelled at her kids on a tough day? Where's the *real* Proverbs 31 mom? Would she please stand? We all need to see her so we can judge her supposed "perfection."

Allow me to read between the lines of this chapter. First

> You're probably doing better than you think you are.

of all, she did not write this chapter in

Proverbs about herself. If she had, I can imagine that it would have looked quite different. As moms, we rarely see ourselves the way others see us; we rarely see ourselves the way God sees us. We are far too quick to criticize ourselves and highlight our imperfections. I can almost guarantee you, Momma: you're doing better than you think you are.

Regardless, King Lemuel wrote this chapter about what <u>his mother</u> had taught him regarding relationships with women and how to find a good wife. {Side note: as moms, we have a huge responsibility to help direct our sons and daughters in relationships. Don't leave it up to chance! Talk about it. Frequently. Build an open dialogue about dating and relationships—even if it's awkward. And don't do all of the talking. Let them open up and ask questions without fear of dismissal or overreaction.}

So what was this SuperMom's secret? Bible scholars aren't entirely sure she was a real woman. She might have been a conglomeration of godly traits from several women the King or his mother knew. Here's the thing: I don't think it matters much if she was real, or one person, or several amazing moms put together. What matters is that she knew one thing we all need to know: she needed help from God.

If you have the time, read the chapter again, and this time pause on verse 30. This is where her secret lies: she feared God. Her strength didn't come from all of her juggling of her household tasks, or having it all together, or being the mom who could do it all with perfectly styled hair and lipstick in place daily. She knew her strength came from the Lord.

In case you don't already know: you can never be the mom who has it all together. You can run yourself ragged until you are flat on your back in your bed, and you will still never live up to the standard you set for yourself—without help from above. Your strength isn't going to magically renew by taking a nap. Your ability to juggle your schedule isn't going to be relieved by saying "no" for an entire week. Naps are helpful; so is saying "no" sometimes. But your strength comes from the Lord, Momma. He is the ONLY One Who can help you be the mom, wife, friend, daughter, or sister that you need to be.

Reflections:

I don't know a mom who doesn't struggle with a stressful schedule sometimes. Some seasons are worse than others. Are you in a season right now that finds you lacking strength? Are you seeking strength from zoning out on social media or hiding out under the covers when you should be digging into the Word? Start today. Get on your knees and ask for help and supernatural strength.

Additional Reading:

-Psalm 55:22, 18:32, Isaiah 40:31
-Proverbs 16:3, Matthew 11:28-30
-Isaiah 64:6, Psalm 18:30, Ezekiel 16:14
-1 Peter 3:3-4, 2 Corinthians 12:9
-Luke 10:41-42, Hebrews 4:15-16

# Leah

*"If you feel you are inadequate, worthless, or not enough, you didn't get those ideas from God."*     -Lisa Bevere

LEAH WAS A "SuperMom" who probably never realized just how "super" she was. Her story starts in Genesis 29.  Read Genesis 29:16-32. As you may recall, God had promised Abraham that his descendants would be more plentiful than the stars in the sky.  Leah was one of the vessels God used to make that promise a reality.

Unfortunately, her wedding day was not one for the cover of bridal magazines. She was a pawn in a scheme to trick Jacob into marrying her first—before he could marry her beautiful sister, Rachel.  And to make matters worse, Jacob loved Rachel; he thought he was marrying Rachel.  Surprise! And talk about being the "third wheel." Poor Leah was hated, and I can only imagine that she wasn't thrilled about the situation either.

But over and over in the story of Leah, it is

clear that God saw her. God loved her. From the day she was born, God had a plan for this SuperMom, and no scheme by her earthly father or her unloving husband was going to stop God's plan for her.

Another thing is clear throughout the story of Leah: she wanted to be loved and cherished by her husband more than anything else. She was willing to go to almost any lengths to earn his attention and affection. Did she realize her efforts were fruitless? Read Genesis 29:33 through to Genesis 30:21. I'm fairly certain that, with each pregnancy, her hope was reborn. Hope...that was deferred time and time again.

As moms, we may not try to earn affection or affirmation from others by bearing children like Leah did. We may not even lack affection from our husbands. I pray your husband loves you more than Leah's did! But that doesn't exclude us from the constant comparison and measuring we engage in to seek attention and affection from others—be it other moms, our bosses, our husbands, our own mothers, or our friends. We have lots of ways, don't we? We buy a new outfit and hope someone notices at church on Sunday. We turn in our work early to our bosses and hope for praise in return. We seek affirmation everywhere, but we fail to notice the One

> Our inherent need for affirmation can only be filled by the One Who sacrificed everything He had to show us His love.

offering us EVERYTHING He had to show us His love.

See, Leah was already loved beyond measure by the God Who created her. While she was busy waddling around searching through baby name books, her Father was there, offering His love and affection to her. He was the Source of her deepest need.

Mommas, you will never be satisfied from the affection and affirmation your husband can offer. You will never be satisfied from another cute outfit hanging in your closet. You will never be satisfied by a plaque that names you "Employee of the Month." You will never be satisfied by the compliments of your friends. You will only find true affirmation and affection that satisfies your soul from the One Who has loved you from your very first heartbeat.

Reflections:

Take a moment and consider your own need for affirmation. Where are you seeking it from? It takes brutal honesty with ourselves to recognize that we are often seeking validation from sources that cannot satisfy.

Additional Reading:
-1 Samuel 16:7, Isaiah 55:8-9
-Ephesians 2:20, 2:10, Isaiah 62:3
-Song of Solomon 4:7, 2:10, Psalms 34:5
-Proverbs 31:25-26, Psalms 139:13-16
-Luke 1:45, Psalm 46:5

# Martha

*"The world clamors, 'Do more! Be all that you can be!' But our Father whispers, 'Be still and know that I am God.'"* -Joanna Weaver

THE NEXT TWO "Supermoms" are, like others in this book, not confirmed mothers in the natural sense. However, their stories are just like those of many moms—including me! So regardless of whether or not they birthed children, these "sister supermoms" have much to share, and I believe there are lessons we can learn from their stories.

Martha is my mom's name. She's despised the name since before I was born, and for decades she's gone by the nickname, "Marti," because she liked it a little bit better than her given name. However, one of my mom's favorite verses in the Bible is John 11:5, which states that Jesus loved Martha. To be completely honest, I think I'd love it if there was a verse in the Bible that said, "Jesus loved Becki." I know He does, of course, but to see it written in print—even if it was meant for an entirely different Martha—would be so special! The verse refers to Martha and her siblings— Jesus loved all of them. Not more than you and me, just uniquely—but the fact that she is mentioned first in the list of her siblings holds some significance if you are aware of the personality traits she is known for.

Read Luke 10:38-42. Martha may not have been a mom in the literal sense, but she certainly acted like I do most days of the week. If I'm not cooking a meal, I'm doing laundry, writing a grocery list, cleaning bathrooms, or scrubbing dishes. The work is NEVER done! My Nana always used to say, "There's no rest for the weary!" If that saying isn't for moms, I don't know who it's for. Martha and I are just the same. My "to-do" list is never completely done; when I've crossed everything off my list, I enjoy the feeling of accomplishment for approximately 2.2 seconds before my brain begins formulating another list.

The very idea of throwing out my "to-do" list ignites a spark of anxiety in my heart almost immediately. Throw it away? We won't have clean clothes tomorrow! No one will eat! If you're a mom, you know very well the chaos that ensues when it's dinner time and there's no food on the table. If I don't get the groceries, who will? These are not theoretical concerns; these are realities of motherhood. But Jesus told Martha that there was something more important than her "to-do" list. And in a gentle, loving way, He encouraged her to throw her list away and focus on what was truly worth her efforts. Doesn't He do the same for us?

Now does that mean Jesus wants us to ignore the laundry, groceries, dishes, and meal plan? Not necessarily. (Although that sounds glorious, right?) Instead, I think He meant that if she had focused on the most important thing FIRST, the rest would fall into place. Think of the last time you spent quality time with Him early in the day. How did the rest of your day go? Better, right? When we focus on the most important thing—spending time in His presence, worshiping, and digging into His Word—we see our "to-do" list with fresh eyes. We can see things through His perspective. And then, suddenly, it's not just doing dishes. It's worship—while you sing along and scrub the grease off of the breakfast dishes. It's not just a trip to the grocery store. It's a 15-minute conversation with your Creator on the way. It's not just folding laundry, it's a prayer meeting as you fold towels and bring your children before your Heavenly Father. Everything that you have to accomplish as a mom looks like a divine appointment when your eyes are focused on Him first.

> Everything that you have to accomplish looks like a divine appointment when your eyes are focused on Him first.

So today, lean in close as He whispers to you those same words He spoke to Martha: "Choose Me first. Let Me change your agenda for today. Don't stress, precious daughter. Give Me your list. We can do it together."

Reflections:

Are you a list-writer? Even if you aren't, if you're a mom, you've got a mental list a mile long. When was the last time you put Him first —not just to "check Him off" your list, but rather to truly seek Him first? What did that look like?

Being busy is a choice. It seems unavoidable to us sometimes, and I am definitely not immune to the pull of "Go! Go! Go!" all the time. But our Savior wishes we would just BE. What are some things you can say "no" to in order to leave margins for being still in His presence?

Additional Reading:

-Psalm 37:5, 46:10, 1 John 2:17
-Matthew 11:28-30, Proverbs 23:4
-Ecclesiastes 3:1-22
-Philippians 3:13-14, Psalm 37:7
-Luke 12:27-28, Matthew 16:24-26

# Mary, the Perfume Waster

"In sweet abandon, let me be spilled out and used up for Thee." -"Broken and Spilled Out," Steve Green

AS WAS MENTIONED before, there is no clear indication that this "SuperMom" was actually a mom. What we do know is that she was part of a family that Jesus dearly loved. Can I tell you a secret? *Jesus dearly loves you and your family too.*

Read John 12:1-7. Although the Bible isn't clear on much of Mary's history, we know she saw her brother raised from the dead. She saw a funeral transformed into a celebration party! Her actions in the events following this amazing resurrection are proof of her unshakeable faith in Christ.

When I think about Mary's story, I think about my mom's fine china. She inherited it from her mother, and my Nana told me many stories about saving her pennies to buy the pieces individually. The set is a gorgeous cream color with tiny pink roses scattered all over. The gold trim makes it "hand wash only" and I can count on my fingers how many times it's been used in my lifetime. Mom (and her mother before her) saved it for special occasions ONLY.

Mary had a perfume that was very expensive—like fine china. Some say it may have cost a year's worth of paychecks. I don't know about you, but the Clinique perfume I wear didn't cost even one of my paychecks, never mind a year's worth. Again, we don't have a lot of history on this purchase; was she wealthy? Was it a gift? It's hard to say. But the point is this: it doesn't matter. If I have a Coach purse, it doesn't matter how I got it—it's still expensive!

Mary took that precious perfume—likely the most expensive item she owned—and poured it on Jesus' feet. In an act that likely took less than ten minutes, she had "wasted" a year's worth of paychecks, anointing Jesus' feet. She didn't hesitate or save any back for herself. She gave it all to Jesus.

And, beyond that, this extreme act of worship was done without any prompting or request from anyone. As Micah Wood described in a recent message he preached: it was "undemanded devotion." She offered her Savior her most prized possession, freely. Her surrender was tangible. It went far deeper than perfume. It was an outward expression of her heart's great affection.

What is the thing you value most? For most moms, it's probably not a *thing*, but rather our marriages, our children, or our time—treasures far greater than mere perfume. And, if we're honest, the people and relationships we value most are often the hardest to surrender to the Savior. We hold our children close with clenched fists, afraid of entrusting them to the One Who created them. We fill our time—usually impulsively—without pouring a single moment out at His feet. But what does that sort of surrender look like in the here and now? It looks like faith; it looks like staying in that spiritual state of surrender while we physically go about our day. It looks like bringing every hope and dream for our children to His capable hands and turning their precious souls over to Him. It looks like abandoning worry and fear for their safety and holding onto His hand instead, knowing He loves them far more than we ever could. It looks like running to Him in prayer even while we're running to the grocery store. It looks like turning over every thought and care and stress and trusting Him instead. It looks like dropping our very hearts in His lap. And resting while He works.

In a beautiful exchange, He takes our cares and gives us courage. He takes our fear and gives us faith. We show our adoration for Him by bringing Him

> In a beautiful exchange, He takes our cares and gives us courage. He takes our fear and gives us faith.

every precious thing we hold dear, every stress that threatens our peace, and every dream our hearts can dare to hope for. Like the best daddy you can ever imagine, He scoops up the broken pieces of our treasures, glorying in the surrender of our souls, and breathes life into our mess.

Reflections:

What is it that you are clenching onto with white knuckles even now?  Is it a job? A relationship? A child? What is stopping you from releasing it even now?

Mary's gift was an outward act of inward surrender.  What can you surrender to your Savior as an act of worship and adoration?

Additional Reading:

-Luke 9:23-24, Philippians 2:5-8
-Galatians 2:20, James 1:22
-James 4:10, Romans 12:1
-Genesis 22:2-14
-Matthew 6:33, 1 Chronicles 16:29-31

# The Shunammite Woman

"Prayer is acknowledging and experiencing the presence of God and inviting His presence into our lives and circumstances." -Stormie Omartian, *The Power of a Praying Parent*

BEFORE THIS SUPERMOM became a mother, she used the resources available to her to serve Elisha, the man of God. She welcomed him into her home and fed him a hearty meal every time his schedule brought him to their area. But that wasn't the extent of her hospitality; she actually received permission from her husband to have an extension built onto their home where Elisha could sleep when he was in town. She literally built him a "home away from home." Read 2 Kings 4:8-14. There are many nuggets of truth we can mine from this SuperMom's story, but this first one is huge: our homes can be a "home away from home" for men and women of God as well as those who have yet to begin a relationship with Him. Hospitality is a ministry. Your kitchen table can be a pulpit, an altar, or a refreshing well for those worn down from the struggle. You are capable of changing lives in your own dining room—it only requires a heart that is willing.

> Hospitality is a ministry. Your kitchen table can be a pulpit, an altar, or a refreshing well for those worn down from the struggle.

But this dear lady's willing heart was harboring a pain many mothers (or would-be mothers) may relate to. Read 2 Kings 4:15-17. She had long given up hope of ever having a child of her own. She was done praying. She was done crying. She was done begging God. She had buried her hurt deep down in a place where she hoped it would be hidden forever. She couldn't bear the thought of that pain rearing its ugly head ever again.

But Elisha promised her that in a year, she would be holding a son. Her response revealed that he had resurrected the long-buried hope she had forsaken. See, this promise was different coming from a man like Elisha. This wasn't a kind remark from a well-meaning friend. This was a statement from the man of God. His words meant she had reason to believe again. She had reason to prepare a nursery again. She could once again browse the maternity section at her favorite stores. But she knew what this meant. It meant vulnerability. It meant exercising her "faith muscles" in a way that opened her up to grave disappointment one more time.

Can I tell you a secret? If you are already a momma, or if you are praying for a baby to fill your waiting arms, there is a great vulnerability in the act of believing for a miracle. There is potential exposure to hurt anytime we step out in faith. But when we dare to believe, God takes note. He knows what it costs for us to

> When we dare to believe, God takes note.

dig out those forsaken dreams, dust them off, and lay them at His feet just one more time. He does not ignore your exercise of faith— regardless of how feeble and tired it may be. Read Hebrews 11:6. The reward for your faith may not look exactly like you expect, but rest assured, Momma. There WILL be a reward.

So this precious SuperMom had her son a year later. I imagine that he grew up knowing exactly who Elisha was. I'm sure his momma shared the story at bedtime, just like I share birth and baby stories with my children. It seems as if it all worked out—a perfect happy ending.

But the story continues as we read on in the passage (read 2 Kings 4:18-37.) Her boy was helping his dad in the fields and he suffered some sort of sudden illness. His dad couldn't be bothered, and sent him to his mother. The thoughts that went through her mind in those terrifying moments were probably similar to the Israelites' as they said to Moses, (paraphrase) "Why did you bring us out of Egypt just to let us die in the desert?"

She had to have been thinking, "God, why did you give me the desire of my heart just to let him die so young?" But let me assure you of something: she may have thought that for a moment or two, but she did not indulge this line of thinking for any length of time. As soon as her miracle child took his last breath, she began to act. Her faith had been realized once, and she was not about to wallow in despair now. She knew the God of miracles, and she knew just the man who had given her the promise in the first place. She called for a donkey and went immediately to Elisha. Read 2 Kings 4: 25-30 again. Notice in verse 30 the adamancy in her words. She REFUSED to leave until Elisha agreed to go with her. There was no burying her hope this time. Her faith was bigger than that now. She knew what God could do and there was no doubt in her mind that the same God who revived her barren womb could revive her deceased child. She didn't settle for Gehazi, Elisha's servant going with her. She didn't settle for half of her promise. She wouldn't move an inch until she knew the man of God was going to come. Her miracle depended on it; her child's life depended on it.

I don't know what you're believing for, Momma. I don't know how big of a miracle you desperately need. But I know the One capable of providing a miracle for you. And I know that He honors faith. It may take days, or months, or years of faithful prayers, but He is the God of the impossible and He wants to show Himself strong in your life. Don't give up when the situation seems hopeless, dead, or long forgotten. Take hold of faith as your lifeline and don't give up. Only God knows how the prayers of tenacious mothers have moved the hand of God.

Reflections:

Hospitality seems to come natural to some of us and not so natural to others. What can you do to increase your influence through the means of opening your home to others?

What hopes and dreams have you hidden away in your heart for fear of being hurt?

What miracle are you believing God for right now? Have you begun to give up hope? How can this momma's life stand as a reminder to you that nothing is impossible for God?

Additional Reading:

> -Exodus 14:10-14, Numbers 21:4-5
> -John 10:10-11, 2 Timothy 1:7, 2 Chronicles 16:9
> -Matthew 19:26, Luke 1:37, Matthew 17:20
> -Jeremiah 32:17, Genesis 18:14, Malachi 3:6
> -Romans 8:18, 1 Thessalonians 2:13, Hebrews 11:1

# CONCLUSION

Hebrews 11 gives the Bible "in a nutshell." The writer describes the many heroes of the faith who form the "cloud of witnesses" that Hebrews 12 refers to. I have always pictured that cloud of witnesses as an arena full of screaming fans, cheering us on as we run the Christian race. I think, to some extent, that is true. But recently, I heard a different explanation for the many heroes of the faith that have gone before us. I want you to picture every one of the SuperMoms in this book as standing still in that arena. They stand as testaments to what a life of faith looks like. Their lives and their stories, detailed in Scripture, cheer us on from the pages of the Living Word of God—not just from a heavenly arena. They stand as witnesses; if they can live lives of unparalleled faith in God, so can we. It's not always easy, as you well know. It wasn't always easy for them. But they held on in faith, and they saw the God of the impossible do the impossible in their days. And if you stand strong in faith, Momma, you will see the God of the impossible do miraculous things in your life, too.

# About the Author

BECKI ROGERS is a wife, mom, teacher, podcaster, and blogger. After growing up in Maine, Becki and her husband Tom now live in Mississippi with their two children, Asher and Ryleigh. Becki is very involved with her church, where she serves on the worship team and leads a Bible study group for moms.

# FOLLOW

## Not {Quite} SuperMoms:

FACEBOOK: Not Quite SuperMoms

INSTAGRAM: @notquitesupermoms

www.notquitesupermoms.com

Did you love this book? Tag @notquitesupermoms in a selfie with the book to be featured on the Not Quite SuperMoms social media pages!

# ACKNOWLEDGMENTS

This book would never have happened without my Father's guidance and wisdom in the writing. This isn't MY message to moms. It's His message to moms and I'm simply the privileged messenger.

My husband and my children have sacrificed so much for this book to be published. There have been countless late nights, early mornings, and grab-your-own-dinners so that I could keep my focus on this work. Tom, I could never have done this without your support! I love you with everything I am.

My church family has cheered me on every step of the way. Greg and Sharrah, I love you guys and The Victory Church. Our church family means the world to me.

My parents have always been my biggest fans. Dad, I cried the day you told me you couldn't believe that my SuperMoms ministry was reaching moms all over America. Mom, you are the cheerleading captain of the SuperMoms Team and I love and appreciate you more than you could ever imagine.

Shelley, you are an inspiration to me and I absolutely love doing life with you. Words cannot express how much I appreciate all you have invested to help me make this book a reality. You are a wealth of knowledge and a fountain of grace, and I cherish our friendship.

To my students who did a great deal of Bible referencing and spot checking for me—I owe you all an A+. You are incredible kids and I was blessed to be your teacher.

# NOTES AND REFLECTIONS

Made in the USA
Columbia, SC
16 October 2022

69550916R00062